DATE DUE

EELS

MARINE LIFE

Lynn M. Stone

Rourke

Publishing LLC
Vero Beach, Florida 32964

www.rourkepublishing.com

PHOTO CREDITS: All photos © Marty Snyderman

Title page: *Like tiny vacuum cleaners, fish called gobies clean a moray eel.*

Editor: Frank Sloan

Cover and interior design by Nicola Stratford

Library of Congress Cataloging-in-Publication Data

Stone, Lynn M.
  Eels / Lynn M. Stone.
    p. cm. -- (Marine life)
  Includes bibliographical references and index.
  ISBN 1-59515-438-8 (hardcover)

Printed in the USA

CG/CG

Rourke Publishing
1-800-394-7055
www.rourkepublishing.com
sales@rourkepublishing.com
Post Office Box 3328, Vero Beach, FL 32964

TABLE OF CONTENTS

Eels

Eels are long, slippery, fish that look like snakes. Unlike snakes, eels breathe through **gills**. And, because they are fish, eels have fins.

Many fish—and even some salamanders—with long, snake-like bodies are commonly called eels.

Eels look like snakes, but they are fish, not reptiles.

Moray eels are among the more than 700 **species** of true eels. More than 100 species of moray eels live worldwide.

The electric eel, for example, has a long body like a snake. But it is not a true eel. Rather, it is a close relative of the knifefish.

True eels are unusual among fish. Instead of being covered by scales, eels are covered by a coat of slime.

Morays are among the largest and best known eels.

Eels swim easily through water and between rocks.

Eels have flattened tails to help them swim. Eels can swim backward nearly as well as forward. That ability helps them slip into narrow cracks between rocks.

What Eels Look Like

Most fish have a series of separate fins. True eels have a long, low fin along their back. That fin joins with what would normally be a tail fin to make one long, continuous fin.

Eels have a long fin along their back.

DID YOU KNOW?

A few kinds of
morays have short,
rounded teeth.

Moray eels have wide mouths and jaws. They are often seen with their mouths wide open by divers. But the moray is not threatening.

Morays generally have sharp teeth, like the dragon moray's fearsome fangs.

The moray's open mouth lets it pump water over its gills.

A green moray's teeth are needle sharp.

Morays average about 5 feet (1.5 meters) in length. The smallest moray is the redface, just 8 inches (20 centimeters) long. The largest morays are more than 10 feet (3 meters) long.

DID YOU KNOW?

Morays are among the most colorful eels. Their bright colors often match their surroundings on coral reefs.

The beautiful marine ribbon eel has an extremely flat body—just like a ribbon.

Where Eels Live

For the most part, the 600 species of eels are **marine** fish. They live in the Atlantic, Pacific, and Indian oceans.

Some eels swim into **brackish** water. A few species spend most of their lives in fresh water. But as adults, they **migrate** to sea to lay eggs. Young eels return from the sea to fresh water to grow up.

DID YOU KNOW?

Eels spend much of their time hiding among rocks or in sand and mud.

A jewel moray hides on the bottom of the Sea of Cortez, Mexico.

Hidden in ocean sand, a clown snake eel in Papua New Guinea shows only its head.

Predator and Prey

Eels are **predators**. The animals they hunt are their **prey**.

Eels eat a variety of small marine animals, including small fishes. Garden eels eat plankton animals that drift by their burrows.

Eels do most of their hunting at night. They have poor eyesight but an excellent sense of smell.

A moray leaves its den to hunt.

The Eel's Life Cycle

True eels hatch from eggs. The first stage of life outside the egg is called the **larva**.

Eel larvas look little like adult eels. They are tiny, ribbon-like creatures. They have clear bodies, like glass. They drift with other plankton animals as they grow.

Eels become adults (large picture) only after going through a larva stage.

A diver carefully feeds a California moray.

Eels and People

Eels are captured and eaten by people in many parts of the world. Eels are not, however, a popular treat in America.

Divers often see moray eels when they visit coral reefs and old shipwrecks. Morays and other large, toothy eels rarely bite people. Big eels are usually dangerous only if they feel threatened.

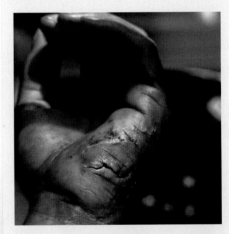

A diver shows the wound made by a moray bite.

Glossary

brackish (BRAK ish) — a mix of fresh and salt water

gills (GILZ) — organs that allow fish to take oxygen from water for breathing

larva (LAR vuh) — an early life stage in many animals, including eels

marine (muh REEN) — of the ocean

migrate (MY GRAYT) — to make a long journey during the same seasons each year

predators (PRED uh turz) — animals that hunt other animals for food

prey (PRAY) — any animal caught and eaten by another animal

species (SPEE sheez) — one kind of animal within a group of closely related animals, such as the *green* moray eel

Index

Further Reading

Hirschmann, Kris. *Moray Eels.* Thomson Gale, 2002

Rothaus, Don P. *Moray Eels.* The Child's World, 1995

Websites To Visit

www.enchantedlearning.com/subjects/fish/printouts/eels.shtml

www.whozoo.org/fish/teleosts/eels.htm

About The Author

Lynn M. Stone is the author and photographer of many children's books. Lynn is a former teacher who travels worldwide to pursue his varied interests.